AF265258

JOURNEY TO THE PAST:

boy to man

Lesedi Manyike

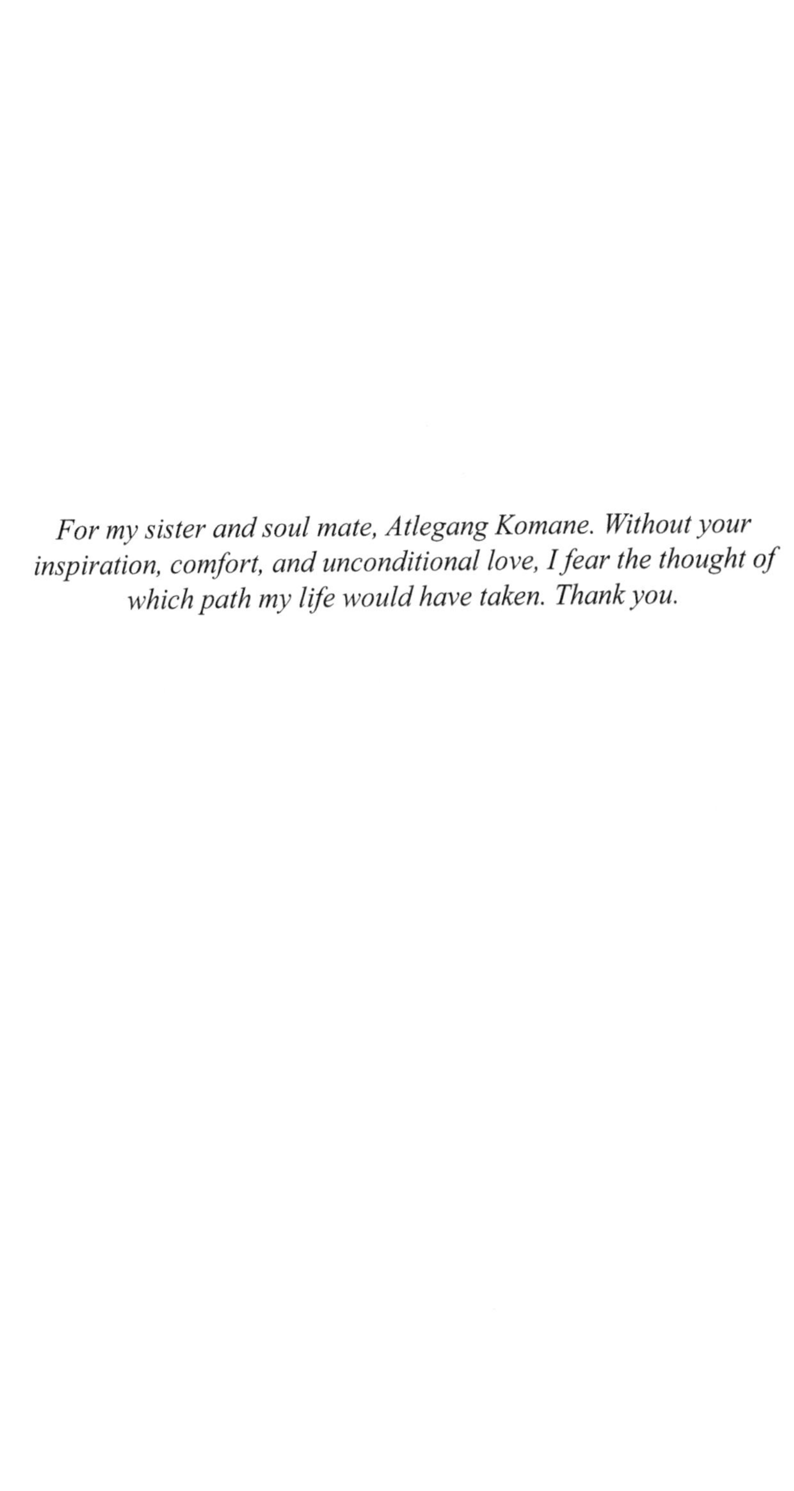

For my sister and soul mate, Atlegang Komane. Without your inspiration, comfort, and unconditional love, I fear the thought of which path my life would have taken. Thank you.

For more information regarding the title, general queries, or to book an event, contact:
mbuzi@lesedimanyike.com
http://www.lesedimanyike.com
alternatively;
mbuzimanyike@gmail.com
linktr.ee/mbuzimanyike

Cover illustrations by Cherlsy Mbire
Illustrations by Lilita Mandita

Paperback ISBN: 978-0-6397-5526-7
eBook ISBN: 978-0-6397-5527-4

First Edition: February 2023

Contents

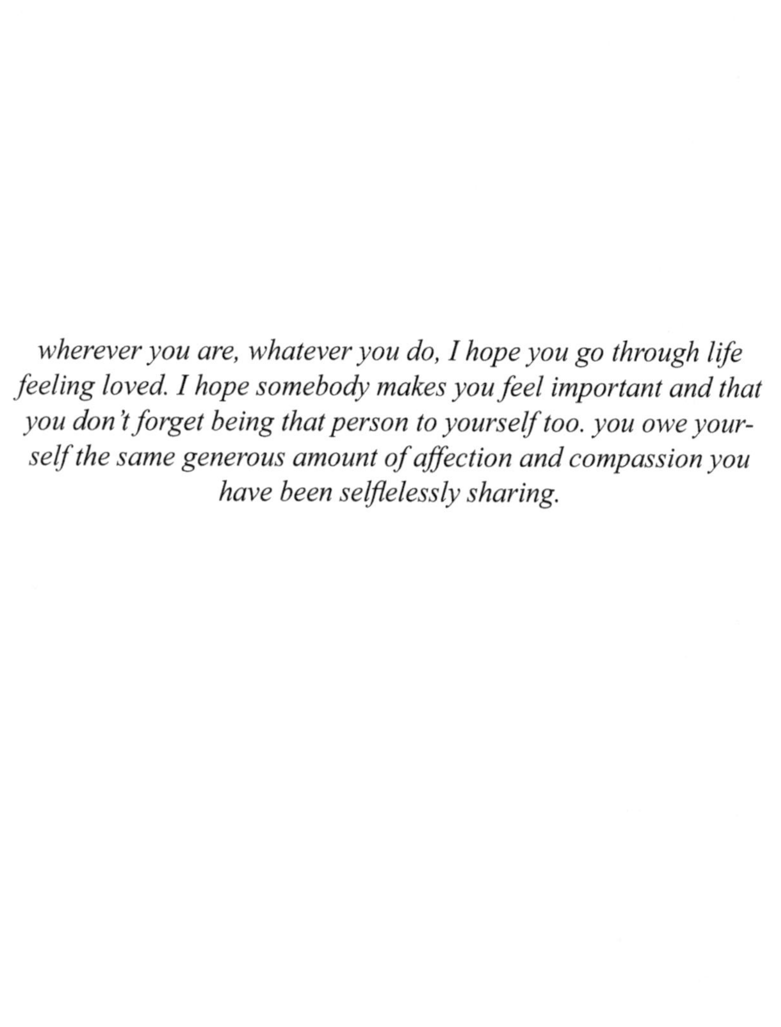

wherever you are, whatever you do, I hope you go through life feeling loved. I hope somebody makes you feel important and that you don't forget being that person to yourself too. you owe yourself the same generous amount of affection and compassion you have been selflelessly sharing.

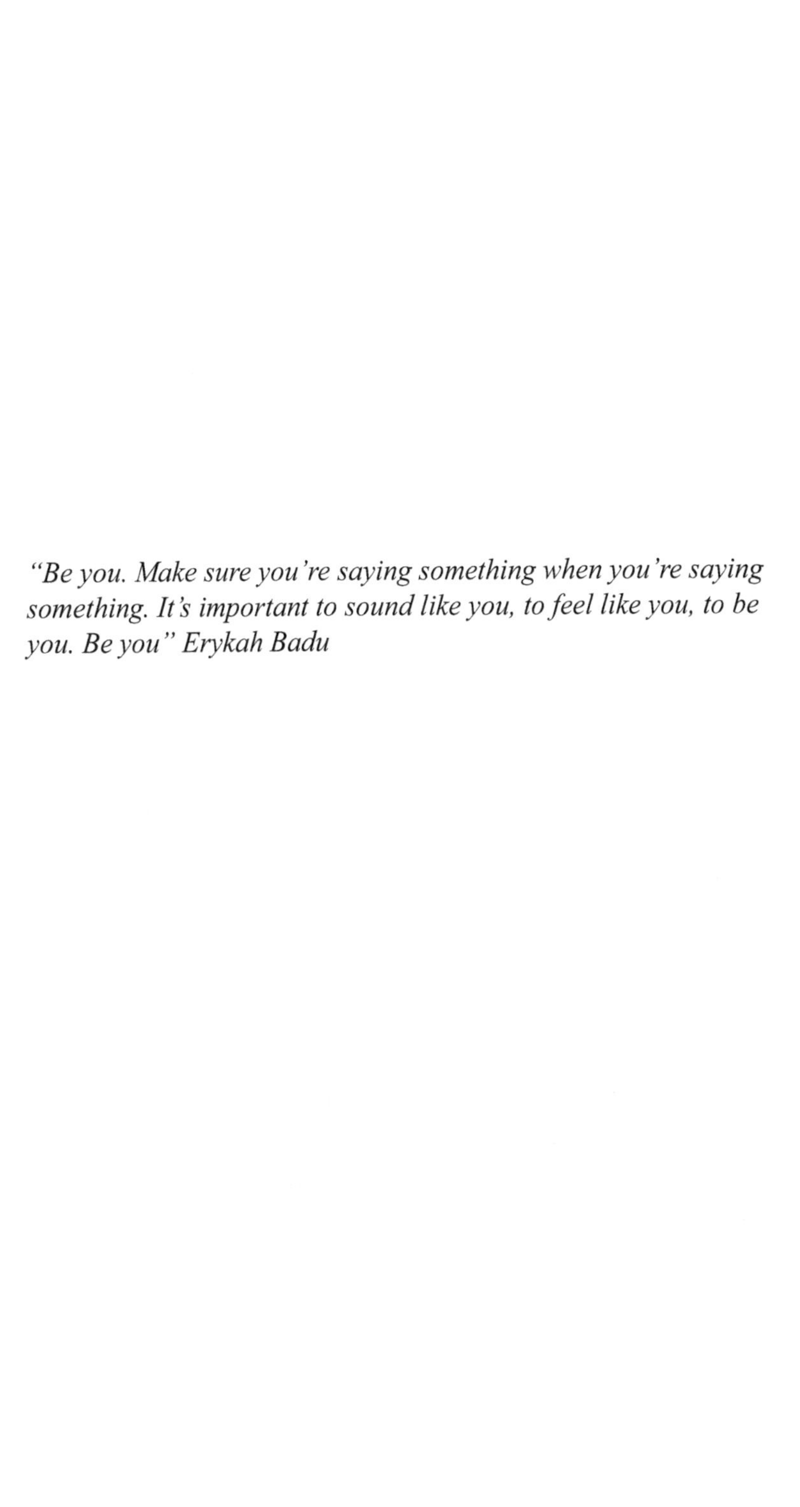

"Be you. Make sure you're saying something when you're saying something. It's important to sound like you, to feel like you, to be you. Be you" Erykah Badu

Author's note

When I entered 2022, my ultimate goal was to heal and learn how to love myself. Setting myself up for such was a challenge, as it was relatively hard to find tools that would aid in the journey. That is when I decided to heal through my poetry. As I started with the first poem, I realized the depth of my experiences. I could not help but think about what someone else might have gone through, the tears they might have cried, and the dark holes they might have found themselves in. I realized that Journey to the past is more than just a collection of poems that visualize a man's coming of age journey, but a collection of poems that have the potential to heal any reader.

Deciding to be vulnerable in front of the whole world is something I have thought about doing for many years, as I believe I could help men and boys around the world understand that it is okay to be vulnerable, the bad days are just part of life, and crying is normal. But as I continued paging through my past experiences, I wanted to narrate them in such a way that they evoke healing amongst men specifically. My biggest wish is to help other men open up, heal, and live happier lives. This anthology seeks to create a generation of men who have a healthy relationship with themselves. This book is open to all, but is written with the intention of healing and inspiring boys and men around the world. *All spelling, capitalization, punctuation, and other grammatical errors are intentional.* ***TRIGGER WARNING: Abuse, self-harm, sexual abuse, bullying.***

Act I
(0 - 13 years old)

The beginning

♈

"push…
push…
come on push…"

Those were the very words that
filled the delivery room as she,
the mother of five geniuses and a half
cracked her hips to spit out two exact opposite
yet identical twins into a world of
cursed lands and one-sided opportunities,
looked up to the doctor in pain and agony.
Pain that was desired to at least be mundane
as this was her fourth physical attempt
at reminding herself that she,
in a world administered by a being that carries a pipe
and by invisible laws that permit him to be
in a higher tax bracket,
is a woman of worth.

At exactly 16.06,
she was freed.
Free from the pain of carrying around
an offspring she herself was not sure would
make it out alive.
This was her last chance
at proving to the world that she,
as an invisible woman existing in
a world of appreciated men and
unseen women
has a voice of her own,
but to prove to her husband at most that she
too was a woman –
a woman who did not deserve the beatings,
but the love only a man can give.

(years later)

49 full moons later
at age 6 there he was,
I.
Existing in a home led by a drunkard
though controlled by her,

the woman who was deemed weak
with abuse wrapped in a cloth that mimicked love
and a father's guide as the dominating thought

cause' he had yarned for it
he stood in front of the mirror,
toes longer than his fingers
knees so close to each other
he often used them as a reference for intimacy,
head as huge as the globe
and skin that glowed with darkness.
He failed to see beyond his imperfections,
and all he saw was a reflection of the words
that dominated his hours

"skinny"
"black"
"awkward"
"unmanly"

At age six
he stood right in front of that mirror,
naked but dressed by the words the world
used to define him.
At age six right in front of that mirror,
his non-existent confidence walked out the door
and self-hate was birthed,
and placed comfortably
on a chair
and ate a meal his ancestors had prepared for those
he had permitted at his table of life.
That was the beginning of a slow
painfully painless journey to a future
that was yet to be defined.

At age 6 he had learned to hate himself
before he was taught the basics of self-love…

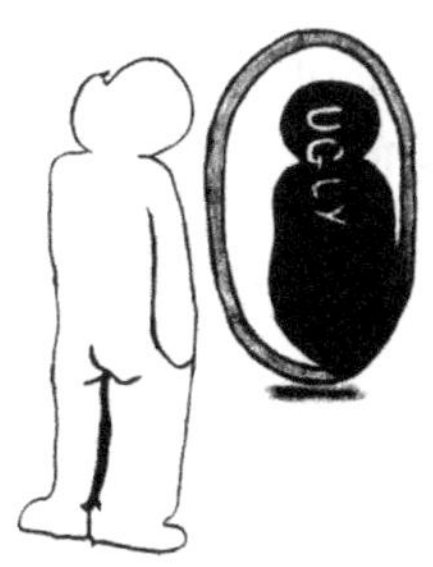

The next two years

♈

The next full moon, the first leaf hit the ground as he entered the great green gates of the place he had no idea was about to be his new home. He sat behind a tiny desk and awkwardly smiled as birth givers and caretakers excitedly waved at the 32 tiny beings that occupied the classroom. Moments later the show was over and a boy his age and nearly his height was placed next to him and he introduced himself, *my name is Remobetswe Molefe, what's yours?* And his first official friend kilometres away from home,was made.

Break time was often spent alone, though some days were better than others as they were spent with his brother and his friends, and some days were spent hopping from one group to another, but on most days, he sat alone squeezing his juice box empty waiting for break time to be over until one graceful day, an unfamiliar female figure approached him and breaktime never the same again.

See, growing up in a family dominated by women made it easier
for him to connect with girls...women, though, his peers saw this
as some sort of weakness cause' no boy wanted to be seen playing
with girls –

"you are gay."
"why are you always playing with girls and not boys?"
– comments his peers made but these unfamiliar female figures
were always there, ready to bark and bite and as time swept by,
these unfamiliar figures had taken him in and became his new
source of protection on the grounds, he did not know had a fire
that was waiting to capture and destroy him.

After days of being fearful of that foreign land
that stood high and proud within those tall great green gates,
he was finally able to take a bite of his brown buttered bread
and finish his meal, because the taste of fear in his young mouth
had made a graceful exit.

Home

♈

The daily commute was never the easiest.
Seven a.m. heading north – school
five p.m. south – the bar
and by seven p.m. the car reeked of alcohol
while he sat in the backseat with his twin,
frightened by the array of possibilities
that come with being on the road with
an intoxicated human being.

Some days were better than others
but the worst days were
the cold winter afternoons spent at school,
alone, waiting for father.
Mother rarely played much of a role
as her daily commute was in direct contrast to theirs.

So, if father knocked off early enough to ditch traffic
in hopes of being the first professional that made it
out the hood yet early enough to
Pat's bar in the orange afternoon,
the boys would be inches away
from accepting that school
had turned into their refugee camp.

He was,
smart enough to use his father's
work-related technology equipment,
yet the direct meaning of home was still to be discovered
so the thick cobweb the internet exposed
became the closest thing to the meaning of home.
With father threatening to kill mother,
they went head-to-head
shoving blade-like words down each other's throats
while the two boys attempted to block the noise
using the television,
and trying to enjoy the supper made with love
and quickly,
he grasped the basics of survival.

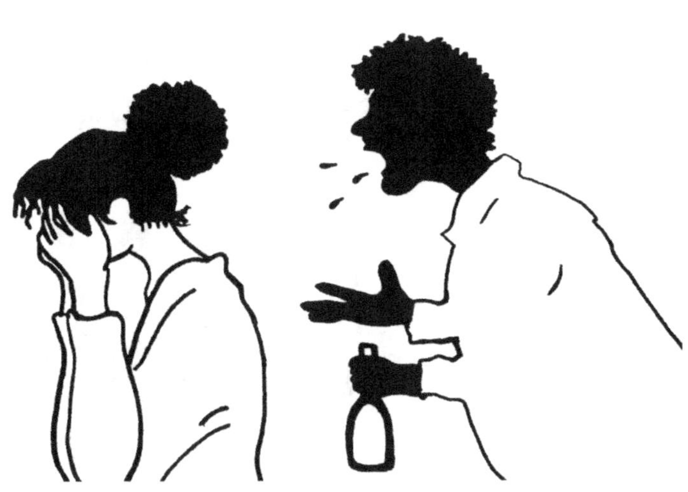

Match days were below the barrel as the winning team
determined their fate.
Step one; call father. Tell him to change
his regular commute,
it's been infested by the men in blue –

*"no intoxicated being
wishes to be in the cold hands of the men in blue"*
Step two; prepare two hot plates of meat and carbs

"don't forget the tub of chili!"
Step three; wait. hope. pray the yellow team
takes the cup cause'
in an expectedly unexpected turn of events,
the lion awakens, shaking the lioness to core.
Pounding, pulsing
evoking palpitations
while necklaced with the paw
as alcohol-laced saliva
dripped from its mouth,
ready to bite,
the woman he vowed
to love and cherish
in the presence of
her devastated father…

But the days that failed to succeed
to the list of horrible days were those
that occurred after a death nearing argument.
Being showered with mind-blowing vacations
mirrored covering
a wet and open wound,
while leaving the boys in the care of guardians
that left their families to
mother a damaged woman's offspring.
Watching mother's upside down
inside out smile
made no difference
as she too shed a tear
while receiving phone calls
from her two baby boys,
as she danced
in the arms
that mimiced a loving touch
but stung when the rest of the world looked away…

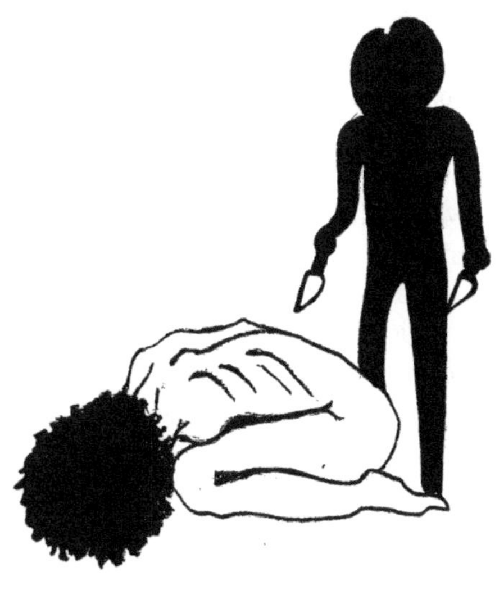

10

♈

At age ten his reality had been set to stone,
as living in a world that constantly
criticized him for finding refuge
in female figures,
any step he took was rooted in considering
what the bully might say next.
He found his masculinity to be threatened and
questioned when he found himself
naked in front of his uncle,
as he touched his knees as though he was a prostitute
and snaked his way up.
Confused by the encounter,
he found himself making terms with this
as he believed was the way of life.
He believed God starred down in awe
because the man who he had looked up to
touched him in a manner
that God had approved of and this,
was yet another experience he believed
was just part of life's norm.
So, he kept his mouth shut and went down
on his knees to thanks to the most high.

Flashbacks and nightmares were forced
to be repressed cause' how dare he
be traumatized by life's norm.
How dare he be captured in the darkness
that took over his body
like death looming over a fresh corpse,
but how dare he expose his dirty body to the world
as it was now occupied by his uncle's fingerprints.
So short-length pants and t-shirts
were buried at the back of his wardrobe,
and that was the sad ending
to wearing clothes,
he wanted to wear.

"cover up," his mind said,
"don't let them
see the cracks and burns
your body carries…"

Being a boy

♈

At this point he had yarned
to be given a manual
on how to be a boy,
cause' being and acting like one
was synonymous
to a final examination,
he had not prepared for.

The mirror became his biggest enemy,
as his drunken abusive father
and periodically available maternal uncle
were never around to guide him
through the ways of being a respectable boy,
so, the closest thing to guidance was comparison.

His walks mimicked
those who surrounded him,
his lingo developed
as daily migration took over
and stance was influenced by the coolest kids.

He became a sponge in an ocean
of diverse characters and soaked up
the different personality traits in hopes
of touching base with what he would be comfortable
labelling as an identity for himself.

Being a boy
became his sole mission
while he was surrounded by girls and women
who assured him that he was boy enough,
though the lessons grasped from the teacher of
comparison worked hard enough to make him aware
that he was rapidly walking away
from his masculinity.

And slowly,
he began to cave in,
giving birth to an alternate identity
that was at least socially acceptable and
mimicked genuine happiness.

Slowly,
he began to lose himself
while trying to hold on
to the last bits of his masculinity.

Big world

♈

With his reality being defined by comparison
in a cold home controlled by alcohol
and led by depression,
the following stage of his life meant
he would be exposed to an advanced level
of insecurities and premeditated bullying.

High school.
Those two words brought shivers down his spine
but hope to his weary mind.
Career aspirations and future considerations
became his mind's new rollercoaster,
confused by this new stage
reality and the subconscious state of mind
failed to be set apart.

The green grounds situated within
the big green gates of hope
had developed into invisible battlefields
that stretched beyond
a naïve being's comprehension,
and he found his torn backpack sitting
uncomfortably on his thighs as he waited
for the white flag of approval
so, he could, run.

Run as fast as he could and never look back.
Memories of an empty lunchbox
and being evacuated from the girl's playground
flashed before his intellect as he skimmed
through photographs that commemorated
the past six years of unrest.

The feeling of being baptized in a pool of
uncertainty washed over his skin when
a sign of the possible ending pain
was brought to the light of day,
then fear of the unknown
became his current recurring trigger.

High school.
those two words forced him to
invite the mirror back into his life
cause' he believed his masculinity needed a revisit,
as the self-acclaimed 'big world' situated
outside those big green gates
would make him prone
to an advanced level of bullying.
Bullying so well thought through
it was ready to destroy a boy that was not
masculine enough-

Though,
he believed bullying was a part of life
and had received God's signal of approval,
so how dare he fear what God had approved of
so, he fell to his battered knees
and gave thanks to the most high.

Tears ran down his cheeks
as his heart pounded at the rhythm
of a rolling stone,
he weakly carried himself
up and out those big green gates of hope
and into the big world of judgment.

With lessons grasped from comparison
in his right,
and derogatory terms that defined him
in his left,
his mind could not escape
fear of the unknown
and familiar feelings
of approaching failure.

High school.
Will he ever conquer the big world
will he ever be masculine enough
to make it past the bullying,
will he ever, be boy enough.

Act II
(14 - 19 years old)

Puberty

♈

13,14
puberty strikes and the headquarters go crazy,
dick grows a few inches longer
and hopes of finding a love interest are raised.
Voice grows deeper and unknown confidence
finds itself stepping up.
Like a rare miracle,
life seems to be getting better by the hour.

It's the first day in the self-acclaimed big world
and his mother is not there to hold his hand
as he walks through the big blue gates
on the sunniest slopes in town.
Mother was not there to help him eliminate the creases
from his shirt nor help him remove
dandruff from his shoulders.
Oh, and father did not give one damn
about how straight his tie was
nor how polished his shoes were,
but this was his first day in high school
so, he had to man up and do it all on his own
cause' how was this day any different
from the day he learned to wrap his school books
at age eight.

Forced growth was his form of survival
in a family occupied by women
who had fair knowledge of the fundamentals
of raising a boy,
so, like the process of fermenting African beer
his growth was dependent on the sun's heat.

At exactly twenty minutes past seven,
his heart and a fast-paced djembe drum
shared characteristics as he entered
those big blue gates.
Seeing familiar faces calmed his racing mind
but he could not escape the scary thought
of how his short beige school pants
exposed his uncle's fingerprints,
on his clashing skinny knees.

Would the egos within the big blue gates
know what happened to him,
or would their focus be shifted to his
lack of masculinity
but wait,
puberty had struck so did that mean
his masculinity had finally made peace with him
and decided to return home,
back to his weary soul again?
Did that mean the world would finally
see the boy in him?

Three Musketeers

♈

As expected, life became easier.
The two familiar female figures
identifiable in their unique ways
were constantly at arms-length,
ready to hold him down
and form a shield against the dangers
within the big blue gates.
Like the three musketeers,
they conquered
the sunny soles and each day
competed with the previous day's excitement.

At this point,
his uncomfortable sadness,
looming loneliness
and manic meltdowns
were identified as
major depressive disorders
and manic depression.

At this point,
the bullying had developed into
a mockery of a boy who sought to be depressed so badly,
but the two female figures still held him down
and somehow knew his only meal of the day
was supper,
so, lunch breaks were spent on the
dying green grass
on the sunniest slopes in town
over an exchange of laughter
and toasted slices of white bread.

The grounds had become a haven
for him,
and waking up every morning was through
the subconscious contribution of the two
female figures that held him down.
Though despite this unity,
he found himself growing physically weaker
as the ocean of loneliness consumed him
with every breath he took.

Feeling numbed by
the overwhelming waters,
sharp razor blades
became the closest thing
to feeling.
Reasons for letting go
were justified by the day,
yet the pressure of proving to life that he
was indeed ready to be a man
kept him from snapping his neck.

With somewhat knowledge of his mental battles
the two female figures showed strength
by pushing him far enough from the cliff,
but the trying and crying
took over his worn-out body,
and pushed him far enough
to gush down two handfuls of pills...

Measure of a man

♈

A man attempting to end his life contributes to the measure of a man, cause' no man wants to be looked at through a lens that makes him appear weak. As he rose from what he hoped was death all the figures that led him to that point surrounded him as tears coated their cheeks, while chanting silent prayers.

The first face he caught glimpse of was his mother's.
Oh, mother, sweet precious mother. But how dare you send him off to school without giving one damn if he had breakfast or not, allowing the abuse to take over and becoming the monster you once feared, never uttered the words *I love you* nor opened your arms for a hug...

Yet she stood on the left side of what he hoped was his deathbed, weeping and chanting silent prayers.

To the right was another female figure he looked up to but had pushed him away when age entered the bones and requested for seriousness in her life, *sister*.

The closest thing to a mother and influence in friendship. One of the women, if not the only woman who cared enough to study his highs and lows but after abandoning him in a
sea of self-confusion and empty fields of foiled fear when he needed her most, there she was on his right weeping and chanting silent prayers. *How dare she?*

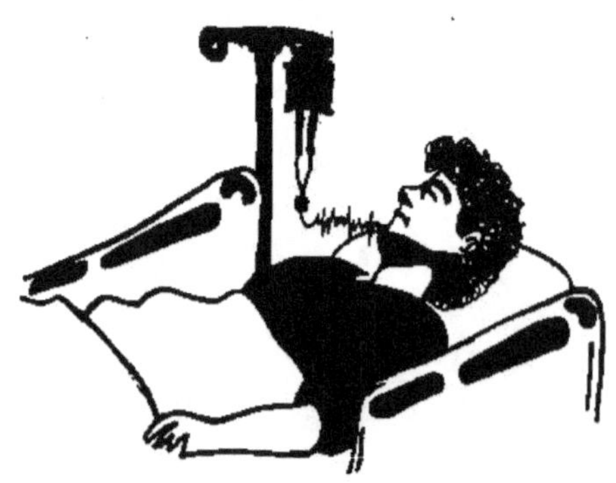

They say sisters are a man's second mother
but one was estranged from him,
the other he feared to the core
while the last,
his favorite had abandoned him.

Clearly, early death was not his birthright
as the array of failed suicide attempts
and the last that neared success
left him feeling like there was no end
and that was it,
his reality was a loop of
endless pain.

Measure of a man,
what needed to give for him
to stand in front of the mirror and say,
I am a boy.
Would tagging along notorious bullies
and engaging in the sport he hated most
be the thing that drives him the furthest,
or would his heavy contribution
to the ever-growing drug culture
help him redefine his masculinity.
What toxic trait did he have to posses
to prove to the world that
he was boy enough?

Self-harm was of no assistance
and this alternate identity
made no difference.
Changing walks and
hanging with the cool kids
made it worse,
so, what would a skinny depressed boy
need to do to prove to the world
that he was indeed ready to be a man.

*"When will the
world finally accept
that I am a boy,
and ready
to be a man?"*

Healing

♈

At nineteen,
a montage of his experiences, dreams and hopes
had become part of his visions.
It was failed suicide attempts,
those helpless therapy sessions
and redundant lessons of comparison
that led him to the realization that
he and only he was at the seat
of the train that drove towards his manhood.
Forgiving his mother was a prerequisite
in the true journey from boy to man,
as resentment towards the first woman who touched
and unconsciously taught him the foundations of love
only drove him away from his manhood,
and disconnected him from any being he could ever love.

Not having an active father figure
pushed him to seek council in outside figures
that could fill the gaping void and
guide him through this meaningless war
he had no idea he was a part of.
But, being aware that love stems from
the roots of the roof that sheltered,
his ever growing hate his for his father
had to be laid to rest,
and he acknowledged that forgiveness
cements a man's respectability.

His relationship with the mirror needed
re-evaluation, a closer look
and a good dive in the ocean
cause' self-love and self-awareness
were factors that defined how the world perceived him.
The lessons of grasped from the teacher of comparison
had to forcefully enter the grave
cause' looking at himself through other men
only pushed him away from his true identity.
And in no time, the bloodline of men
who came before him laid
the traumatized and confused
little boy he once was to rest,
awakening the man in him.

Light is promised at the end of each tunnel,
so, like a troubled stream under a bridge
he went flowing to be reunited with other men
who had taken charge of their own journeys.
The end was met and
peace and forgiveness were meals of the day,
the high mountains he had gone by over the years
were recognized as tests that were sought to
evoke the true man in him.
So, for one last time
and with an open heart,
he went down on his knees to
give thanks to the most high.
This time however,
his form of thanks was healing his inner child
and setting his aching heart to rest.
The world's colors brightened and
took on many forms as he carefully
embarked on a journey to the past,
forgiving all the figures who created scars
and assuring beauty to his young fragile reflection.
The journey from boy to man
was a period he recognized as a test that
could either make or break a man,
yet fate was determined by
choices the *boy* made.

Boy to man

♈

masculinity,
muscle density,
a bushy beard
and being feared.
terms and factors
that have somehow found a way of
of defining a man.
this is a song to that boy who cannot hang
cause' his feminine energy and
soft mannerisms remind the gang
of his apparent difference.
that transgender man who's transition
is turned a blind eye upon,
or that man who simply failed
to identify his masculinity in a manner
that makes sense to the world.
that boy who has to hide from bullies,
or had no father to raise him.
this is a song of comfort.

the universe has got a mind of its own
and was ready to consume him,
I.
the boy who hated
the hand that
fed air and loud noises
while trying to find protection
from the apple.
navigating the world with nothing but
a heart full of hope
exposes the body to potentially preventable harm,
but he managed to dodge that bullet.
so, this song sends words of comfort
to that man,
whose gender was questioned
because his weight evoked man breasts
or long hair covered his eye.
this song hugs that man that recognizes
these days as his last
or that man who is ready to get up and try again,
that boy who cries every single night
asking himself if it will ever end.
this song celebrates him,
and commemorates his journey.
this was his form of healing,
embarking on a
 journey to the past; from *boy to man.*

Background

Act I
(0 - 13 years old)

The beginning

♈

The title of this poem is self-explanatory. This was the beginning of everything, life before the pain, the commencement of the pain, and it all takes us back to the day I was born. In this poem, I critically look at my mother and her contribution to society through her family while bringing forth the abuse she endured from my father. The lack of my father's mostly emotional presence in our lives is also suggested while the poem itself does not give away too many details that may spoil the following poems.

Full moon references
2003 – 12
2004 – 13
2005 – 12
2006 – 12

20 – 22:   My mother had told me once that the stress she endured during our pregnancy specifically, led her into believing we would not make it out alive.

23 – 31:   The abuse my mother was experiencing at the time was no secret, well at least to us. In all honesty, I have never seen my parents being affectionate towards one another. Looking at their relationship through a critical lens left me believing that my mother may have not wanted as much as five children but felt the need to prove her existence through us, and maybe just maybe my father would stop seeing her as less of a woman by bearing children for him.

40 – 41:   As a young boy, I had always wished for my father to be active in our lives. As much as we saw him every day and he took us to school, I could not help but wish for him to teach me how to put on my tie, how a man is supposed to act, or even how to speak to girls. He was always out but the times he was in the house, he was either too busy with work or too drunk to stand us.

42 – 71:   Growing up, I hated myself. The word itself does not emphasize the amount and extent of the then existing hate. The mirror was the least of my favorite items as looking at it would remind me of how the bullies were right; I was too skinny, my head was too big and my skin tone was too dark. The bullying got to an extent where I was asked if I was sick or not, if I ate or not.

My mind was beyond my body being the way it was due to genes as my family did not fail at reminding me about how skinny I was everytime they saw me naked, leaving me to question if I was really sick. So, when I realized that everyone around me could see how imperfect my body was, I stopped wearing shorts, t-shirts, and any form of body-revealing clothes altogether, unless I had no other way out.

The next two years

♈

This poem is one of my favorites in the entire collection. In this poem, I have a look at my journey through friendship by putting the very first friend I made in school in the spotlight, alongside the friends I had made in grade one, and friends that would later carry on the journey with me until the end. Friendship is one thing that has given me hope and kept me going. My friends had a very huge impact on my life as I was growing up. Had I not met the people I could call friends during the first two years of primary school, I refuse to imagine how my story would have unfolded. This poem celebrates them.

Additional references

'The big green gates' –

At the time, green was part of my primary school's main colours, the gates and fences were green, and the grass was always green.

3 – 4:   Home had never really felt like home to me so I would constantly find myself hoping any new environment I would find myself in would give me something to hold on to and eventually give me the feeling of being home. Until I got to primary school, and school became my home.

28:         I hated break time. The friends I made were girls, and in our school, girls were separated from the boys during break time which meant I would be separated from my friends. On days the teachers would kick me out of the girls' playground I would either join my twin and his friends or just sit alone. The girls would try to sneak me into the playground, some days we were lucky and some days we were not until the girls finally decided that we look for a spot where the teachers would not have to bother us.

27 – 41:   Coming from an abusive home, with distant siblings and parents I did not have someone to reach out to or proactively protect me, but these friends protected me. I did not know how to speak up or stand up for myself, but these friends would do so for me. When bullies tried their luck with me, my friends would deal with the matter and that person would not be seen anywhere near me again. I think the most beautiful part about this entire experience is that from my perspective, I did not see this as girls protecting a boy but rather as a group of friends protecting one of their friends. It was my friends that made school a home-like and very warm and safe space for me.

Home

♈

Writing this poem was one of the hardest pieces I have written. I had to dive and dig deeper into the experiences I endured at home. In this poem I take readers into our home in hopes of helping them understand the dynamic, the type of person my father was and our day-to-day experiences

1 – 20:   My father worked in Pretoria Central and school was in Centurion, so our daily commute was linear and straightforward. Home-time was not the best but a few good memories live with me every day. After work (usually any time after 15:30), my father would collect us from school and we had to make sure we were waiting at the gate or he would leave us behind. We then hit the freeway and turned left into the main road that would lead us to a tarven (an inn or pub) in Tembisa he spent most of his time at. He was always in a rush to get to the tarven after work so us being late to the car was as good as a death wish, sometimes he would just not collect us. My mother worked in the opposite direction towards school so on days we were left at school it would be a struggle to get us back home because either my mother was working late or traffic would prevent her from even attempting, so we spent a lot of afternoons waiting at school till very late.

21 – 26:   Before my father got sick and lost his job due to his disability (2011, I was 8), I was very fond of using his work equipment. From his computer, to laminator machine, printers etc. He worked at Telkom so he had all kinds of technology related equipment and I, a curious boy, was always ready to see what would happen if I pressed 'OK.'

27 – 32:   Not a day would go by without my parents getting into some sort of fight, so most evenings were spent trying to block their noise with the TV's volume while we tried to have our supper.

31 – 51:	My father adored soccer with everything in him, so match days, especially when his favourite team played were a big deal. He supported the 'Kaizer Cheifs' team and should it lose on game night, we were in for a treat. He mostly watched the games at the tarven and after 10pm, we would call him to let him know that he should use an alternative route, as the police were always ready to catch drunk drivers on the main road. We then had to ensure that one plate of meat and one plate of pap (traditional porridge / polenta, a staple food for Africans in South Africa), accompanied by a tub of chili that went with all his meals were waiting for him in the TV room. On our unluckiest days, Kaizer Cheifs would lose and home would be turned into a battlefield. On such days, my parents' fights would get so intense that their faces would only be a few centimetres away from each other as they yelled at one another.

58 – 76:   After big fights, my father would shower my mother with random trips to random places and the two would leave us behind. We would call my mother crying, and as young as I was, I could hear the pain in my mother's voice when she spoke to us. The calls would sometimes be too intense for her and she would just hang up as we battled to speak and cry at the same time.

Outside home, my father was a very respected and respectful man so no one would suspect that such a man was capable of abuse. I recall my mother saying she used to stop him by threatening to tell his colleagues about what he does – he was an angel when the world looked at him, but a monster when they turned away.

10

This poem is the shortest within the entire collection, yet it holds one of the experiences that not only confused me as a young troubled boy, but shaped me and my perspectives on a lot of thimgs. When I wrote this poem, I believed that this particular experience within the entire book would empower others to not only to speak up, but also to protect and support those around them.

2 – 4:   From the first grade, I have always had to answer to people who asked me why I had female friends. I sometimes lost friends, and possible love interests due to this matter and the bullying that came along with the questions was sometimes unbearable despite me being used to it.

5 – 9:   When I was ten years old, I was molested by someone I could call my uncle. I do not know if he was my uncle or not as this happened at my great-grandmother's place and it was a family gathering. So, it would only make sense if he was my "uncle." I did not know what to do nor what to say about it, so I just kept quiet.

10 – 20:   I grew up Catholic and was a deep follower of the Christian religion. At some point I was even an altar server (the priest's assistant during mass (church service)). I grew up believing God knew and saw everything that happened to and around me, and that alone gave me more reason to be quiet.

27 – 38:   After this encounter, I hated my body even more and I officially stopped wearing shorts and T-shirts forever. Unless I was forced to, like at school.

Being a boy

This poem is one of the only poems in the collection that made me very emotional while drafting it. It made me think about the times I would look at my peers who were able to befriend other boys and wonder what was wrong with me because it was hard for me. It made me think about the times I would listen to the other boys tell us what their fathers taught them and the jokes their fathers told them, and I would sit and listen to them in awe... Asking myself if I was any different, if I was not deserving of having an active father to teach me what BEING A BOY meant.

8 – 17:   Growing up, I would find myself fascinated by the boys who had active fathers in their lives. Seeing their fathers hug and support them was something very odd for me. I would carefully study these boys then I would act, dress and speak like them because I believed their behaviour was what their fathers taught them and approved of.

22 – 35:   After what my experiences had taught me, I was able to create an alternate identity for myself using certain character traits I had picked up from observing the boys who had active, loving and supportive fathers. Slowly, I was able to avoid myself…and everything that came with being myself.

Big world

♈

When writing this poem I changed many parts, the message included, because I was not sure if I was ready to be raw about my relationship with my mother. Looking at this poem, I take readers down my memory lane, as I conclude my last years in primary school and introduce my high school years. Leaving primary school was not easy, as I was in great fear of losing my friends. The greatest fear I had to carry with me as we walked out the gates was the thought of being around people who were older than I was, and given my past experiences I did not do well around older people I did not know. I was afraid of being bullied and I knew the bullying I would endure in high school would be ten times more than what I had endured in primary school, and to say I was terrified of high school is an understatement. I had no one to speak to or even tell I was being bullied. I sometimes thought it was okay to never say something because being bullied was something I was used to my entire life and at some point, it felt normal...

1 – 9:   After watching movies, hearing stories and reading books about high school I was convinced I would be the perfect target in high school

15 – 18:   At first, school was my haven, my escape, but as I slowly got to understand what was happening, I realized that school was a horrible place – or at least for me it was. My best days and worst hours were influenced by events that occurred at school.

23 – 28:   My primary school years evoked mixed feelings; from going to school without having had breakfast or without lunch, to the days I would not want to participate in activities that required us to wear home clothes because we barely had new clothes or shoes. As much as I was fearful of what might have happened in high school, I could not wait to go to high school as I hoped it would get a bit better.

35 – 45:   From a young age, masculinity has always been a thing for me. I did not really have as many male friends as I hoped to have nor any active male figures in my life so I would constantly ask myself if the way I dressed, spoke and acted was "boy-enough."

58 – 65: When I left primary school, I was on defence mode. I had studied how my bullies often looked like, how they dressed, walked and even spoke. So, when I was able to spot someone who came across as a bully, I would quickly remove myself. The sad part about this behaviour is that I battled with trusting someone who had qualities that remind me of one of my bullies.

66 – 70: As I left primary school, I could not help but think about myself in every way possible. I kept asking myself if I was ever going to be boy-enough, I kept asking myself if I would ever amount to the other boys who had male friends and never got bullied… I kept asking myself, "when will my body change?" I kept asking myself if I would ever get to a state where I would not be worth bullying…

Act II
(14 - 19 years old)

Puberty

♈

During this stage of my life, I was beyond excited. My friends would tell me that my voice was getting deeper, which had a positive effect on how I looked at myself. I thought that would be the moment the world would start seeing the man in me. This poem introduces readers to the two friends that held me down. They were aware of the mental battle I was going through, they knew what was going on at home and they gave me comfort. This poem is special to me, because as I was reading it before publishing, I could not help but think about how these two special friends contributed to me seeing the light at the end of the dark tunnel I had found myself in. This poem also brought some sort of sadness because I thought at this point my mother had recognized her distance at this point, and I hoped she was maybe going to do something about it. 'Puberty' is a poem that celebrates the two friends who helped me define friendship.

9 – 23:   By the time I was already in grade two I had learned to take care of myself. From wrapping my own school books, getting myself ready for school, and polishing my school shoes, but I wished my mother would have gotten up a bit earlier than she normally did just to prepare our breakfast and ensure our stationary was all ready for our first day in high school. Sure my mother had a helper who assited her...but it's just not the same. I thought she would at least want her proof of existence to somehow look perfect or maybe we already were. I will never know…

24 – 29:   It was quite unfortunate that my mother, aunt and sisters had to raise the first large numbered generation of boys in the family and well, I do not think they are to be blamed for how it turned may have out. Most of the time, my cousins and twin were left in my older cousin and I's care because I was "more mature."

30 – 49:	I was always worried that people would know what happened to me, so I would distract them with my art, butterfly personality and my curious and mature mindset. Sometimes I would behave impulsively – I was known to be the problem kid in class.

43 – 49:	When puberty hit, I was just waiting for it. That thing that all men had and made the world see them as men. I waited for it, and waited, and waited…

Three Musketeers

♈

This poem alone has a very special place in my heart. I take readers down the road I walked when I got closer to my two special friends. I also openly share the mental health related issues I dealt with at the time and the positive impact these two friends had in my life at the time.

1 – 11:   When I got to high school, I was very nervous but I stared to calm down as I saw familiar faces. I was then put in the same class as two friends I was quite close to and it only got better. The three of us were all different but our personalities complimented each other, we even went as far as giving our little yet significant union a name – The Three Musketeers. The two knew me very well, they knew when I was okay and they knew when I was not okay. We cried together, we laughed together, we comforted each other, and I found myself experiencing some form of love I had never experienced outside home. For the first time in a long time, I felt safe.

12 – 18:   When I was in grade eight one, of my teachers referred me to the school psychologist and soon after that my classmates would pass around jokes about me "faking depression." This continued for quite some time and well, to others it stuck with them for a long time and they would constantly ask me questions. I continued seeing the psychologist in grade nine, and when she learned that I was now harming myself by cutting my wrists she referred me to a psychologist and psychiatrist on a more professional scale. I was then diagnosed with major depressive disorders and other mental health related illnesses. And from there on my reality was trying to survive through the prescribed medication.

19 – 29:   In grades eight and nine, we barely had much to eat at school. My Father would only give us R250($13) each a month. I remember we would buy food only after school since the food sold on the streets was much cheaper but the R250 was also used to get other essentials we needed but had no access to because my mother would just tell us she did not have money. Breakfast was a game of hope; we had to hope there was either some bread we could eat or leftovers from the previous night. What humbled me was that every day my friends always happened to have extra lunch so, we would always have something to share. I would at least have something to eat until supper time.

35 – 41:   Throughout the time I was first diagnosed I was very suicidal and numb, so I would cut myself in hopes of feeling something...

46 – 52:   Somehow my two friends knew I was not okay, so they spent as much time around me as possible and they would do anything and everything just to make sure I was at least smiling and distracted in that moment. We did not really have an actual conversation about it but they always tried to prevent me from committing suicide, but I attempted either way.

Measure of a man
♈

I think this poem visualizes one of the most traumatic experiences I endured. I will never forget the smell of the hospital I was admitted to when I attempted to commit suicide, or the things said to me or about me. I will never forget hearing the sounds of people fighting for their lives in the ICU. I will never forget how my family members called my act selfish and tried to make me feel guilty. I will never forget how alone I was during that time, and how I wished my attempt was successful.

1 – 4:	It is no secret that society barely offers a safe space for men to be vulnerable, so hearing a man attempted to commit suicide or succeeded becomes a bit of a taboo. I vividly remember the looks all the nurses gave me as they walked past my hospital bed and while reading my medical record. A few nurses even came to me and told me that if I were to sit with a group of people and they told me their problems, I would understand how my experiences are just a drop in the ocean, so I should "be grateful and glad."
22 – 39:	I have always been closer to my third sister, but after her high school days, she slowly started to let go of me. She was the only person that understood exactly how my I felt without a doubt because she lived and grew up in that mad house. With her being able to understand, our connection was beyond our comprehension.
52 – 62:	From the moment I became conscious to the idea that masculinity is the biggest defining factor of a man's manliness, I have always looked at my circles, my family, friends and myself, trying to understand where it all went wrong. I have always been trying to be a man that makes sense to me and the world at large.

65 – 71:   In the midst of my suicidal episodes, I felt beyond helpless. I was clearly not meant to have an early death, self-harm was of no assistance nor was my impulsive behaviour and trying to befriend the cool boys. I was beyond helpless…

Healing

♈

When I decided to write Journey to the past, I wanted to use my poetry as a tool that would aid in my healing journey. I acknowledged that the world does not have enough safe spaces for boys and men to proactively be vulnerable and express their emotions. I wanted my story to be reassuring to that boy or man that feels alone. I wanted my story to be a kind and gentle reminder that they are in fact not alone, and that their experiences are valid. Writing this collection of poems gave me hope that if other men could see me being vulnerable in front of the world, accepting my past, healing from my past and moving on, would somehow motivate them to embark on a similar journey. I wanted this collection to speak to every single young boy around the world, boys that do not feel enough, boys that are confused, boys that are still trying to tap into their identity, boys that do not feel heard. I wanted this collection of poems to be a universal tool for healing. I wanted this collection of poems to heal any reader that opens this book. This poem promotes healing.

10 – 15:   Shortly after I turned nineteen, I looked at my friends, the people in and around my circles and I could not help but see a part of myself in them and their experiences and behaviours. I considered my experiences and opinions and realized I had to forgive my mother as my journey helped me discover that how a man treats his mother gives you an idea of how he will treat his woman of interest and other woman around him.

16 – 26:   Hating my father had taken a lot from me than it did from him, I became conscious of this and my energy had to be shifted. With the shift in energy, I had a deep desire to forgive him. As much as I found council from other male figures who came across as father figures to me throughout my entire life, I needed to accept my father for who he was and make peace with what he did and lack thereof. At the end of the day, he was my father and my peace was on the line. Therefore, *I forgave him.*

27 – 37:   I also realized I needed to love and treat myself in the way I wanted to be treated because I believe that how the world loves, sees and treats us, is a reflection of how we do to ourselves. I needed to be content with myself. I needed to treat myself with so much love and care that the world recognized that I am the writer of my story. At this point, I was ready to love myself again.

51 – 57:   The first step to loving myself was healing my inner child, so I got into the habit of actual prayer, meditation, shadow work and soul searching, and through that was I able to start putting my young hurt forever crying self to rest. I had to give my younger self a warm hug so my life could continue.

Boy to man

♈

When I wrote this poem, I was not writing it for myself. This poem was written for all the boys and men around the world, both the troubled and those at peace. This poem is a celebration of men and promotes masculinity that is rather healthier than toxic. This is a song that celebrates masculinity that accommodates femininity. This is a speech for men who have the platform to influence the foundation of masculinity.
This poem is a message to future generations.

24   "the hand that fed :   My mother
            air and loud noises"

27   "the apple":   My father

- END -

About the author

Lesedi Manyike "Mbuzi" is a poet, performance artist, actor, model, photographer, an all-around creative entreperneur, who made his first appearance on stage as a dancer at the age of five. His love for poetry dates back to grade two when he entered the speech festival held annually in his primary school. In high school, he took his poetry to different art festivals, community centres, and different events with different audiences. His love for the arts as a whole is evident in his work ethic and contribution to the creative economy. His work celebrates lineage, sparks conversations related to mental health, Southern African history and culture, and promotes healing all together.

www.lesedimanyike.com

Acknowledgements

I would like to use this platform to thank my old high school teacher, Mrs. Lennox, for believing in my poetry. When I was in grade nine you called me to your office, made me coffee and allowed me to cry. When we had nothing to eat at school, you made sure that a plan was made. When I wasn't feeling like myself, you allowed me to be. You loved and cared for me like I was your child, and I will forever be grateful for that. I would like to also extend my gratitude to my dance mother, A.K.A Ms. G Mkhosi. In 2015, I joined your dance classes, and you went from my teacher to mother. You have shown me love and support from the day I walked in your studio. You spoke to me like you understood what was going on in my mind even though you may have not. When we went on our trips to the theatre and I had no food, you sacrificed yours just so I could have something to eat. You have always called me your one and only son, and you have treated me as such. Thank you <3

R e s o u r c e s

0861 322 322 –   Lifeline Southern Africa

1-800-985-5990 –   Mental Health America

13 11 14 –   Lifeline Australia

1-833-456-4566 –   Crisis Services Canada

0800 068 4141 –   HopeLine UK

0800 543 354 –   Lifeline New Zealand

0033 145 39 4000 –   Suicide Ecoute (France)

030 44 01 06 07 –   Telefonseelsorge (Germany)
800 86 00 22 –   Samaritans (Italy)

+81 (0) 6 4395 4343 –   BI Suicide Prevention Centre,
                                   Osaka (Japan)

107-0062 –   Tokyo English Lifeline

Websites accessible anywhere around the world

http://www.suicide.org/international-suicide-hotlines.html
(International suicide hotlines)

https://www.imalive.org/
(I AM ALIVE – Online live chat for suicide prevention)

https://www.psycom.net/
(General information and self-assessment about a variety of mental
health issues)

Playlists

*These playlists have been helped me a lot in my healing journey.
On the days I wanted to cry, be alone, to feel something, celebrate,
and all the good and bad stuff, these playlists would not dissapoint
in helping me do so, and I hope they can allow you that platform
as well.*

Scan on Spotify to access the playlists

Mbuzi's Collection: Journey to the past, "peace"

Mbuzi's collections: Journey to the past, "well"

Mbuzi's collections: Journey to the past, "its not over."

Mbuzi's collections: "blessed, by the youth."

In this section of the book, the last section, I want you to write a letter to someone you think needs to recieve the message of this book. This could be your younger self, a stranger, perhaps your brother, your father maybe, and even your sister. As much as I can not tell you what to do with this book, I would love for you to write a letter in this book and hand it to them, and hopefuly they can do the same for another persom, and if you wrote a letter to your younger self you can pass the book on to anyone in need of the message. The moment the last person to recieve this book no longer has space to write another letter, I believe the cycle of healing related to this book would have come to an end.

If you are writing the letter to yourself, I want you to write the letter and let go. If you are writing to anyone else, please let them know that all will be well, and that they need to let go. That is one of the main messages of this book, let it go.

You are going to be okay, okay?

x

My dearest brother Bokang, it has been hard. If there is
anyone on this planet that understands the extent of the
pain we both suffered in that house, it is you.
With mommy being...well mommy, and papa being...
papa, there is so much that was taken away from me
mentally because of their joint experiences and I could
not help but think about your perspective and your hurt.
You being a person that barely expresses how they feel
about certain things left me worried at times. I know
a lot of things made you sad, or angry, but I may have
never understood excatly what was going on in your
mind.
I hope as you have come to the end of this book, the
parts of you that may have been ruined when we were
growing up can be mended.
I pray that wherever life takes you, you can look back at
that house numbered 26 and be able to laugh about the
things we may not been able to laugh about, and pretty
much everything else. We can live our lives now, the
nightmare is over.

Love,
Lesedi.

A letter to: ___________________________

____

____

____

____

____

____

____

____

____

____

____

____

____

____

With love,

____

A letter to: _______________________

With love,

A letter to: _______________________

____

____

____

____

____

____

____

____

____

____

____

____

____

With love,

____

A letter to: _____________________

With love,

____

A letter to: ___________________________

____

____

____

____

____

____

____

____

____

____

____

____

____

With love,

____

A letter to: ______________________

____

____

____

____

____

____

____

____

____

____

____

____

With love,

____

A letter to: _______________________________

____

____

____

____

____

____

____

____

____

____

____

____

____

With love,

____

A letter to: _______________________

____

____

____

____

____

____

____

____

____

____

____

____

____

With love,

____

A letter to: _______________________

____

____

____

____

____

____

____

____

____

____

____

____

____

With love,

____

A letter to: _____________________

With love,

____

A letter to: _______________________

____

____

____

____

____

____

____

____

____

____

____

____

____

With love,

____

A letter to: _______________________

____

____

____

____

____

____

____

____

____

____

____

____

____

With love,

____

A letter to: _______________________

With love,

____

A letter to: __________________________

____

____

____

____

____

____

____

____

____

____

____

____

____

With love,

____

A letter to: ______________________

____

____

____

____

____

____

____

____

____

____

____

____

____

With love,

____

A letter to: _______________________

____

____

____

____

____

____

____

____

____

____

____

____

____

With love,

____

A letter to: _______________________

____

____

____

____

____

____

____

____

____

____

____

____

____

With love,

____

A letter to: _______________________

____

____

____

____

____

____

____

____

____

____

____

____

____

With love,

____

A letter to: _______________________

____

____

____

____

____

____

____

____

____

____

____

____

____

____

With love,

____

A letter to: _______________________

____

____

____

____

____

____

____

____

____

____

____

____

____

____

With love,

____

A letter to: ______________________________

____

____

____

____

____

____

____

____

____

____

____

____

____

With love,

____

A letter to: _______________________

With love,

____

A letter to: ______________________________

____

____

____

____

____

____

____

____

____

____

____

____

____

With love,

____

A letter to: _______________________

With love,

____

A letter to: ______________________

____

____

____

____

____

____

____

____

____

____

____

____

____

____

With love,

____